# Guarding Freedom

# The Perils of Initiative 2025

D M. Juliana

Copyright © 2024 by D M. Juliana

All rights reserved.

No part of this publication may be reproduced, distributed, or transmitted in any form or by any means, including photocopying, recording, or other electronic or mechanical methods, without the prior written permission of the publisher, except in the case of brief quotations embodied in critical reviews and certain other noncommercial uses permitted by copyright law.

# Disclaimer

The content of this book, "Guarding Freedom: The Perils of Initiative 2025," is based on thorough research and analysis. The opinions expressed are those of the author and do not necessarily reflect the views of any organizations or individuals mentioned. This book is intended for informational and educational purposes only.

 The author does not provide legal, financial, or professional advice. Readers are encouraged to seek professional guidance for specific concerns.

All efforts have been made to ensure the accuracy of the information presented; however, the author assumes no responsibility for errors or omission

# Introduction

## A Nation on the Brink

It was the early hours of a chilly morning when the first light of dawn crept over the nation's capital, and an air of uncertainty hung thick in the atmosphere. It was a time of great change, a period of tumultuous shifts and brewing tensions.

Amid the growing clamor for reform and the cries for maintaining the status quo, one initiative emerged from the shadows, promising to reshape the very fabric of American democracy—Initiative 2025.

As a journalist with a deep-seated love for my country's democratic ideals, the news of Initiative 2025 hit me like a thunderbolt. I remember the night vividly, sitting in my small office, the soft hum of the city outside my window as I pored over the documents that had landed on my desk.

The words on the pages were more than mere political proposals; they were harbingers of a profound transformation, one that could tip the scales of power irrevocably.

**The Dawn of Initiative 2025**

Initiative 2025 was the brainchild of the Heritage Foundation, a powerful conservative think tank with a vision of overhauling American governance. Their mission: to centralize authority, dismantle bureaucratic constraints, and streamline federal operations. To many, it seemed like a beacon of efficiency and strength in a time of perceived governmental gridlock and inefficiency.

But I saw beyond the veneer. I saw the echoes of history, the faint but unmistakable outlines of past regimes that had started with similar promises. I recalled my university days, studying the rise of authoritarianism in Germany, Italy, and Russia. The patterns were eerily familiar: the consolidation of power, the suppression of dissent, the erosion of checks and balances. It was as if the past was whispering warnings through the annals of history, urging vigilance.

## A Journalist's Quest

As the weeks passed, I embarked on a quest to uncover the deeper implications of Initiative 2025. I spoke with political scientists, historians, and constitutional law experts, piecing together a mosaic of insights and analyses. Each conversation added a new layer to my understanding, painting a picture that was both complex and deeply concerning.

The initiative's goals were clear: to centralize power within the executive branch, to reduce the autonomy of federal agencies, and to push through significant social and economic reforms. Proponents hailed it as a necessary step towards a more efficient government, but I feared the potential for overreach and abuse of power.

## The Fight for Education

One of the most startling revelations was the plan to reduce the role of the Department of Education. As a product of the public education system and a firm believer in its value, I found this particularly alarming.

I visited schools, talked to teachers and parents, and documented the fears and hopes of those who would be most affected. The consensus was clear: this move threatened to deepen educational inequities and undermine the very foundation of a free and informed society.

## Defending Reproductive Rights

The battle over reproductive rights was another front in this ideological war. Initiative 2025 proposed changes that could restrict access to reproductive health services, potentially rolling back decades of progress. I interviewed women from all walks of life, gathering poignant stories of struggle, resilience, and the unyielding fight for autonomy over their own bodies.

## The Broader Impact

As my investigation deepened, I saw the broader picture: the potential rollback of civil rights, the end of criminal justice reforms, the suppression of free speech, and the economic policies that threatened to widen inequality.

Each aspect of Initiative 2025 seemed to interlock, forming a cohesive strategy that could fundamentally alter the democratic landscape of the United States.

## A Call to Action

One evening, as I reflected on my findings, I realized that my role was more than just a journalist reporting on events. I was a guardian of truth, a defender of democratic values, and my words could rally others to the cause. The urgency of the situation called for more than passive observation—it called for action.

I penned the opening lines of what would become a powerful manifesto: "In these uncertain times, it is crucial for each of us to remain vigilant and proactive. This book is not just a warning but a call to action—an invitation to stand up for the democratic values that define our nation. Together, we can ensure that our democracy remains strong and resilient."

## Transition to the Journey Ahead

With my purpose clear and my resolve steeled, I prepared to take you  my readers on a journey through the labyrinthine corridors of power and policy.

"As we delve into the blueprint for authoritarianism," I wrote, "we will uncover the strategies and implications of centralizing power, drawing on historical examples and expert analyses. Our journey begins with understanding the past to safeguard the future."

And so, with a sense of mission and a heart full of determination, I embarked on the first chapter of this book, inviting readers to join me in guarding the freedom we cherish.

# Chapter 1: Authoritarian Tendencies and Centralization

## The Lure of Absolute Power

In the dimly lit corridors of power, where decisions are made behind closed doors, the lure of absolute authority is an ever-present temptation. Throughout history, leaders have sought to consolidate power, often under the guise of efficiency, stability, or national security.

Initiative 2025 is the latest incarnation of this age-old quest. To understand its implications, we must first explore the essence of authoritarianism and its historical precedents.

# Defining Authoritarianism

Authoritarianism, at its core, is a political system characterized by strong central power and limited political freedoms. In such systems, power is often concentrated in the hands of a single leader or a small elite, with few checks and balances to prevent abuse.

The hallmarks of authoritarian regimes include:

- **Centralization of Power**: Authority is consolidated at the top, often bypassing or weakening legislative and judicial branches.

- **Suppression of Political Dissent**: Opposition voices are silenced through censorship, imprisonment, or worse.

- **Control of Information**: The media is controlled or heavily influenced by the government, ensuring a one-sided narrative.

- **Erosion of Democratic Institutions:** Democratic norms and institutions are systematically dismantled or rendered ineffective.

# Historical Context: Lessons from the Past

To grasp the full impact of Initiative 2025, we must look to history. Authoritarian regimes did not arise in a vacuum; they often emerged in times of crisis, exploiting public fears and uncertainties. Consider the following examples:

- **Germany in the 1930s**: The Weimar Republic, weakened by economic woes and political instability, saw the rise of Adolf Hitler. Promising order and national revival, Hitler systematically dismantled democratic institutions, establishing a totalitarian regime marked by brutal repression and catastrophic war.

- **Italy under Mussolini**: Benito Mussolini capitalized on post-World War I unrest, using nationalist rhetoric and promises of economic recovery to gain support. Once in power, he eliminated political opposition and controlled the media, creating a fascist state.

- **The Soviet Union under Stalin**: Joseph Stalin transformed the Soviet Union into a tightly controlled dictatorship.

Through purges, censorship, and state terror, Stalin consolidated power, suppressing any form of dissent.

## Initiative 2025: The Centralization of Power

Initiative 2025 proposes several measures aimed at centralizing authority within the executive branch. While proponents argue that these reforms will lead to more efficient governance, critics warn of the dangers inherent in such centralization. Key proposals include:

- **Expanding Executive Authority**: Initiative 2025 seeks to increase the powers of the presidency, allowing for greater unilateral decision-making.

- **Reducing Federal Agency Autonomy**: The initiative aims to streamline federal agencies by reducing their independence. Agencies like the Environmental Protection Agency (EPA) and the Department of Education could see their powers curtailed, bringing them under tighter executive control.

# Impact on Checks and Balances

The United States' system of checks and balances is designed to prevent any one branch of government from gaining too much power. By increasing executive authority and diminishing the role of other branches, Initiative 2025 threatens to disrupt this delicate balance. Experts warn that such changes could lead to:

- **Weakened Legislative Oversight**: With Congress's role potentially diminished, the executive branch could act with less scrutiny, leading to unchecked power.

- **Eroded Judicial Independence**: Reducing the judiciary's ability to review executive actions could undermine the rule of law, making it harder to challenge unlawful or unconstitutional policies.

# Bureaucratic Reforms: Efficiency or Overreach?

One of Initiative 2025's key selling points is its promise to streamline government operations. By cutting red tape and reducing bureaucratic constraints, the initiative aims to create a more efficient government. However, history has shown that such reforms can backfire:

- **Loss of Accountability:** Reducing oversight mechanisms can lead to corruption and abuse of power, as officials operate with less scrutiny.

- **Historical Failures**: Similar reforms in other countries have often resulted in increased authoritarianism.

## Suppression of Dissent

Control of information is a crucial tool for any authoritarian regime. Initiative 2025 includes measures that could lead to increased media control and restrictions on free speech:

- **Media Control**: Provisions to regulate the press and control the dissemination of information could stifle independent journalism. Historical parallels include the extensive propaganda machinery in Nazi Germany and the Soviet Union's state-controlled media.

- **Silencing Opposition**: By suppressing dissenting voices, Initiative 2025 could create an environment where only government-approved narratives are heard. This suppression has been a common tactic in authoritarian regimes to maintain power and prevent challenges.

## Educational Case Studies

To illustrate the potential consequences of Initiative 2025, we can look at contemporary and historical case studies:

- **Hungary under Viktor Orbán**: Orbán's government has systematically dismantled democratic institutions, centralized power, and controlled the media.

These actions have led to significant democratic erosion, serving as a modern example of how quickly democratic backsliding can occur.

- **Chile under Pinochet**: Augusto Pinochet's regime in Chile used centralized power and suppression of dissent to maintain control. The aftermath of his rule left deep scars on Chilean society, highlighting the long-term damage of authoritarian governance.

**Call to Vigilance and Engagement**

Democracies do not fail overnight; they erode gradually, often under the guise of necessary reforms. It is up to the citizens to recognize the signs and take action to defend democratic values:

- **Staying Informed**: Emphasize the importance of being aware of political developments and understanding their implications.

- **Active Participation**: Encourage readers to participate in the democratic process, through voting, advocacy, and community engagement.

- **Collective Responsibility**: Highlight the collective responsibility to safeguard democratic values and institutions.

# Chapter 2: Threats to Educational Autonomy

My mind raced with questions about the future of education in America. What would happen to our nation's schools, teachers, and students if these proposals became reality?

## Overview of Educational Reforms

Initiative 2025 proposes significant changes to the educational system, starting with reducing the role of the Department of Education. This section explains the scope and intentions behind these reforms:

- **Central Objective**: The primary aim is to decentralize control, shifting authority from federal to state and local levels.

- **Efficiency and Choice**: Proponents argue that this will lead to greater efficiency, more local control, and increased school choice for parents and students.

## Potential Changes to Federal Oversight

I explored how Initiative 2025 plans to change federal oversight:

- **Reducing the Department of Education's Role:** The proposed reduction in the department's functions and the redistribution of its responsibilities to states and local governments.

- **Funding Changes**: Potential shifts in funding mechanisms, including block grants to states, which could lead to disparities in educational resources and quality.

## Possible Consequences for Public Education

Through discussions with educators, administrators, and policy experts, I considered the potential consequences of these changes:

- **Increased Inequality**: Without federal oversight, disparities between wealthy and impoverished districts could widen, exacerbating educational inequality.

- **Loss of Standardization:** The absence of federal standards could lead to varying educational quality and content across states.

- **Impact on Special Programs**: Programs designed to support disadvantaged students, such as those for special education and low-income families, might suffer from inconsistent funding and implementation.

# Comparative Case Studies

To provide a broader perspective, the chapter examines international examples of decentralized education systems:

- **Finland's Success**: Finland's highly decentralized yet equitable and high-performing educational system, supported by strong local governance and community involvement.

- **Challenges in the United States**: Historical examples from American states that have experimented with decentralization, highlighting both successes and failures.

## Expert and Educator Insights

I spoke with various stakeholders to gather diverse perspectives:

- **Teachers' Concerns:** Interviews with teachers reveal fears about job security, resource availability, and the quality of education they can provide.

- **Administrators' Challenges**: School administrators discuss the potential administrative and logistical challenges of operating without federal guidelines and support.

- **Policy Experts' Analysis**: Insights from educational policy experts on the broader implications of reducing federal oversight and the potential long-term impacts on national educational standards.

# Educational Impact of Initiative 2025

My research revealed the broader implications for American society:

- **Civic Education and Democracy**: The role of education in fostering informed and engaged citizens, and the risks of undermining this function.

- **Economic Consequences**: The potential long-term economic impact of an unequal and underfunded education system, affecting workforce readiness and innovation.

# Chapter 3: Challenges to Reproductive Rights

## The Ongoing Struggle

I walked through the doors of a bustling community health center, where the atmosphere was charged with both hope and anxiety. The center provided essential reproductive health services to women from all walks of life.

As I interviewed the staff and patients, it became clear that Initiative 2025 posed significant threats to these services.

### Overview of Reproductive Rights

Reproductive rights encompass a range of issues, including access to contraception, abortion, and comprehensive reproductive healthcare. Over the past decades, significant progress has been made in ensuring these rights for women across the United States. However, Initiative 2025 proposes changes that could undermine these gains.

## Legislative Changes Under Initiative 2025

The initiative seeks to introduce several legislative changes that could restrict access to reproductive health services:

- **Regulations on Abortion Providers:** Increased regulatory requirements that could force many clinics to close.

- **Restrictions on Funding**: Cutting federal funding for reproductive health services, impacting organizations like Planned Parenthood.

- **Limitations on Contraceptive Access**: Policies that could reduce access to affordable contraception.

## Potential Impact on Women's Health

Through conversations with healthcare providers and policy experts, I assessed the potential impact of these changes:

- **Reduced Access to Services**: Women, particularly those in low-income and rural areas, could face significant barriers to accessing reproductive healthcare.

- **Increased Health Risks**: Restrictions on abortion and contraception could lead to higher rates of unintended pregnancies and associated health risks.

- **Economic Consequences:** Limited access to reproductive healthcare can have broader economic impacts, affecting women's participation in the workforce and overall economic stability.

## Comparative Case Studies

To understand the potential effects of these proposed changes, the chapter examines case studies from other countries that have implemented similar restrictions:

- **Ireland Before Repeal**: The impact of strict abortion laws in Ireland before the repeal of the Eighth Amendment, which led to significant challenges for women seeking reproductive healthcare.

- **Poland's Recent Changes:** The recent tightening of abortion laws in Poland and its effects on women's health and rights.

## Expert and Advocate Insights

I spoke with various stakeholders to gather diverse perspectives on the issue:

- **Healthcare Providers**: Interviews with doctors and nurses who provide reproductive health services, discussing the practical implications of increased regulations.

- **Policy Experts**: Insights from legal and policy experts on the broader implications of restricting reproductive rights.

- **Advocates**: Perspectives from reproductive rights advocates on the potential social and political consequences of these changes.

## Broader Implications for Society

My research revealed the broader societal implications of restricting reproductive rights:

- **Impact on Gender Equality**: Limiting access to reproductive healthcare is a setback for gender equality, affecting women's autonomy and ability to make decisions about their own bodies.

- **Social Justice Concerns**: These changes disproportionately impact marginalized communities, exacerbating existing inequalities in healthcare access and outcomes.

# Chapter 4: Erosion of Civil Rights Protections

## A Fragile Balance

Walking through the halls of a local civil rights organization, I was struck by the palpable tension in the air. Advocates were working tirelessly, aware that Initiative 2025 could fundamentally alter the landscape of civil rights in America. Their concerns echoed those of many I had spoken to: the potential for significant rollbacks of hard-won protections.

## Overview of Civil Rights Protections

Civil rights encompass a broad range of protections designed to ensure equality and prevent discrimination based on race, gender, religion, and other characteristics.

Over the years, landmark legislation and court decisions have advanced these rights, fostering a more inclusive society. However, Initiative 2025 proposes changes that could reverse this progress.

# Legislative Changes Under Initiative 2025

The initiative seeks to introduce several legislative changes that could undermine civil rights protections:

- **Weakening Anti-Discrimination Laws**: Proposals to modify or repeal existing anti-discrimination laws, affecting protections in employment, housing, and education.

- **Redefining Civil Rights Legislation**: Changes that could narrow the definition and scope of civil rights, making it more difficult to prove discrimination.

- **Limiting Federal Oversight**: Reducing the power of federal agencies to enforce civil rights laws and conduct investigations.

## Potential Impact on Civil Rights

Through discussions with legal experts and civil rights advocates, I assessed the potential impact of these changes:

- **Increased Discrimination:** Without robust anti-discrimination laws, marginalized groups could face heightened discrimination in various aspects of life, including employment, housing, and education.

- **Legal Challenges**: Narrowing the scope of civil rights could make it more difficult for individuals to seek legal recourse and prove cases of discrimination.

- **Reduced Enforcement**: Limiting federal oversight could weaken the enforcement of civil rights laws, leading to widespread non-compliance and diminished protections.

## Comparative Case Studies

To understand the potential effects of these proposed changes, the chapter examines case studies from other countries and historical contexts:

- **South Africa Post-Apartheid:** The challenges faced in maintaining civil rights protections and combating systemic discrimination in a changing political landscape.

- **United States Pre-Civil Rights Movement:** The conditions and societal impacts before the landmark civil rights legislation of the 1960s, providing a stark contrast to the progress made since then.

**Expert and Advocate Insights**

I spoke with various stakeholders to gather diverse perspectives on the issue:

- **Legal Experts:** Insights from constitutional lawyers and civil rights attorneys on the broader implications of weakening civil rights protections.

- **Civil Rights Advocates**: Perspectives from advocates working on the ground to protect and advance civil rights, discussing the potential social and political consequences of these changes.

- **Community Leaders:** Views from leaders in marginalized communities on how these changes could affect their constituents and the broader fight for equality.

## Broader Implications for Society

My research revealed the broader societal implications of undermining civil rights protections:

- **Impact on Social Cohesion:** Eroding civil rights protections can lead to increased social tensions and divisions, undermining efforts to build an inclusive and equitable society.

- **Economic Consequences:** Discrimination and inequality can have broader economic impacts, affecting productivity, workforce participation, and overall economic stability.

# Chapter 5: Reversing Criminal Justice Reforms

## The Call for Justice

Standing outside a courthouse, I watched as families gathered to support their loved ones, many of whom were seeking justice and reform within the criminal justice system. Initiative 2025 proposed changes that could reverse recent progress in criminal justice reform, raising significant concerns among advocates and those affected by the system.

## Overview of Criminal Justice Reforms

Recent years have seen significant strides in criminal justice reform, aimed at addressing issues such as mass incarceration, racial disparities, and police accountability. However, Initiative 2025 proposes changes that could undermine these efforts and exacerbate existing problems.

## Legislative Changes Under Initiative 2025

The initiative seeks to introduce several legislative changes that could reverse criminal justice reforms:

- **Reinstating Mandatory Minimum Sentences:** Proposals to bring back mandatory minimum sentences for certain offenses, reducing judicial discretion and increasing incarceration rates.

- **Expanding Law Enforcement Powers**: Enhancing the powers of law enforcement agencies, potentially at the expense of civil liberties and oversight.

- **Reducing Support for Rehabilitation Programs:** Cutting funding and support for programs aimed at rehabilitation and reintegration of formerly incarcerated individuals.

## Potential Impact on Criminal Justice

Through discussions with legal experts, reform advocates, and affected individuals, I assessed the potential impact of these changes:

-   **Increased Incarceration Rates:** Reinstating mandatory minimum sentences could lead to higher incarceration rates, disproportionately affecting marginalized communities.

- **Erosion of Civil Liberties:** Expanding law enforcement powers without adequate oversight could lead to abuses of power and violations of civil liberties.

- **Reduced Rehabilitation Opportunities:** Cutting support for rehabilitation programs could hinder efforts to reduce recidivism and support successful reintegration into society.

## Comparative Case Studies

To understand the potential effects of these proposed changes, the chapter examines case studies from other countries and historical contexts:

- **Norway's Rehabilitation Model:** The success of Norway's focus on rehabilitation and reintegration, leading to low recidivism rates and better outcomes for formerly incarcerated individuals.

- **United States War on Drugs:** The impact of the War on Drugs policies in the United States, which led to mass incarceration and significant social and economic costs.

## Expert and Advocate Insights

I spoke with various stakeholders to gather diverse perspectives on the issue:

- **Legal Experts:** Insights from criminal justice lawyers and reform advocates on the broader implications of reversing criminal justice reforms.

- **Formerly Incarcerated Individuals:** Perspectives from individuals who have experienced the criminal justice system firsthand, discussing the importance of rehabilitation and support.

- **Policy Experts:** Analysis from policy experts on the potential social and economic consequences of these changes.

## Broader Implications for Society

My research revealed the broader societal implications of reversing criminal justice reforms:

- **Impact on Social Justice:** Undermining criminal justice reforms can exacerbate existing social inequalities and undermine efforts to create a fair and just society.

- **Economic Consequences**: High incarceration rates and reduced support for rehabilitation can have broader economic impacts, affecting workforce participation, productivity, and overall economic stability.

# Chapter 6: Curtailing Free Speech and Media Independence

## The Silent Threat

I walked into a newsroom buzzing with activity, where journalists were diligently working to uncover truths and inform the public. However, there was an underlying sense of unease. Initiative 2025 had introduced proposals that threatened to curtail free speech and media independence, key pillars of any democracy.

## Overview of Free Speech and Media Independence

Free speech and a free press are essential components of a democratic society. They allow citizens to express opinions, criticize the government, and access unbiased information. Over the years, these rights have been protected and upheld through legislation and judicial rulings.

However, Initiative 2025 proposes changes that could undermine these protections.

**Legislative Changes Under Initiative 2025**

The initiative seeks to introduce several legislative changes that could restrict free speech and media independence:

- **Regulating Media Outlets:** Introducing stricter regulations on media organizations, potentially leading to increased government control over news content.

- **Restricting Freedom of Expression**: Proposals to limit certain forms of speech deemed harmful or unpatriotic, which could stifle dissent and suppress minority viewpoints.

- **Enhanced Surveillance Powers**: Expanding government surveillance capabilities under the guise of national security, potentially infringing on privacy and freedom of expression.

## Potential Impact on Free Speech and Media

Through discussions with journalists, media experts, and legal scholars, I assessed the potential impact of these changes:

- **Censorship and Self-Censorship**: Increased regulation and surveillance could lead to direct censorship and self-censorship among journalists and citizens, fearing repercussions for speaking out.

- **Erosion of Trust in Media**: Government control over media content could erode public trust in the media, as citizens may perceive news as biased or propaganda.

- **Chilling Effect on Free Speech:** Restrictive laws on expression could create a chilling effect, where individuals refrain from speaking out on important issues due to fear of legal consequences.

## Comparative Case Studies

To understand the potential effects of these proposed changes, the chapter examines case studies from other countries and historical contexts:

- **China's Media Control:** The extensive control the Chinese government exerts over media and internet content, leading to censorship and limited access to unbiased information.

- **Turkey's Crackdown on Free Speech:** The impact of Turkey's restrictive laws on free speech and media, resulting in the imprisonment of journalists and suppression of dissent.

## Expert and Advocate Insights

I spoke with various stakeholders to gather diverse perspectives on the issue:

- **Journalists and Editors:** Interviews with journalists and editors about the potential impact of increased regulation and surveillance on their work and freedom to report.
-     **Legal     Scholars**:     Insights     from constitutional law experts on the broader implications of restricting free speech and media independence.

- **Media Advocacy Groups**: Perspectives from media advocacy organizations on the potential social and political consequences of these changes.

## Broader Implications for Society

My research revealed the broader societal implications of curtailing free speech and media independence:

- **Impact on Democracy**: A free and independent media is crucial for holding power accountable and ensuring an informed citizenry. Undermining these freedoms can weaken democratic institutions and processes.

- **Social Justice Concerns:** Restrictions on free speech and media can disproportionately impact marginalized communities, whose voices are often suppressed in favor of dominant narratives.

- **Economic Consequences**: A free press plays a critical role in economic transparency and accountability. Limiting media independence can lead to corruption and reduce public trust in institutions.

# Chapter 7: Socioeconomic Consequences

## The Ripples of Change

The proposed changes not only threatened democratic principles but also posed significant risks to economic stability and social equity. It became clear that these reforms could have far-reaching effects on American society.

## Overview of Economic and Social Policies

Economic and social policies shape the distribution of resources, opportunities, and services within a society. Initiative 2025 proposes substantial reforms aimed at restructuring these policies, claiming to promote efficiency and growth. However, the potential for increased inequality and economic instability cannot be ignored.

# Key Economic Proposals Under Initiative 2025

The initiative introduces several key economic proposals:

- **Tax Reforms:** Changes to the tax code aimed at simplifying taxation but potentially favoring higher-income individuals and corporations.

- **Deregulation**: Reducing regulations on businesses to encourage investment and growth, with potential risks to consumer protections and environmental standards.

- **Welfare Reforms**: Overhauling welfare programs to reduce federal spending, which could impact support for low-income families and vulnerable populations.

## Potential Economic Consequences

Through discussions with economists and policy analysts, I examined the potential economic consequences of these proposals:

- **Increased Income Inequality:** Tax reforms and deregulation could disproportionately benefit the wealthy, widening the gap between rich and poor.

- **Economic Instability**: Deregulation may lead to short-term economic gains but could increase the risk of financial crises and environmental degradation.

- **Reduced Social Mobility:** Cuts to welfare programs could limit access to essential services, making it harder for low-income individuals to improve their economic situation.

## Social Impact of Economic Policies

The social implications of these economic policies are profound:

- Health and Well-being: Reductions in welfare support could lead to increased poverty, affecting health outcomes and overall well-being.

- Educational Inequality: Economic disparities often translate into educational inequities, as wealthier families can afford better educational opportunities for their children.

- Community Stability: Increased inequality can lead to social unrest and reduced community cohesion, undermining social stability and trust.

## Comparative Case Studies

To provide a broader perspective, the chapter examines case studies from other countries and historical contexts:

- **Austerity Measures in Greece**: The impact of austerity measures on the Greek economy and society, leading to significant economic hardship and social unrest.

- **Welfare Reforms in the United Kingdom**: The effects of welfare reforms in the UK, which have been criticized for increasing poverty and inequality.

## Expert Insights

I spoke with various stakeholders to gather diverse perspectives on the issue:

- **Economists**: Analysis from economists on the broader implications of the proposed economic reforms and their potential long-term impacts.

- **Social Workers:** Perspectives from social workers on the frontline, discussing how cuts to welfare programs could affect the communities they serve.

- **Policy Analysts:** Insights from policy analysts on the potential social and political consequences of increased economic inequality and reduced social mobility.

**Broader Implications for Society**

My research revealed the broader societal implications of the proposed economic and social policies:

- **Impact on Social Equity:** Increasing economic inequality and reducing social mobility can undermine efforts to create a fair and just society.

- **Economic Growth and Stability**: While some argue that deregulation and tax reforms can spur economic growth, the potential risks to long-term stability and equity are significant.

- **Political and Social Cohesion:** Economic disparities can lead to political polarization and social fragmentation, weakening the fabric of society.

# Chapter 8: Strategies for Civic Resistance

## Rising to the Challenge

As I attended a town hall meeting, the room buzzed with energy and determination. Community leaders, activists, and concerned citizens had gathered to discuss how to respond to the threats posed by Initiative 2025.

It was clear that grassroots mobilization and civic engagement would be crucial in protecting democratic values and ensuring social justice. This chapter explores practical strategies for resisting and countering the negative impacts of the initiative.

## Historical Movements and Lessons Learned

Throughout history, successful movements have risen to challenge authoritarianism and injustice. This section reviews some of these movements, extracting lessons that can be applied today:

- **The Civil Rights Movement:** Examining the strategies used to achieve legislative and social change in the face of systemic racism and discrimination.

- **The Anti-Apartheid Movement:** Understanding how international solidarity and internal resistance led to the dismantling of apartheid in South Africa.

- **Recent Protests in Hong Kong:** Analyzing the tactics used by pro-democracy protesters to resist authoritarian encroachments and mobilize global support.

# Grassroots Mobilization

Grassroots efforts are often the backbone of effective resistance. Key strategies include:

- **Community Organizing:** Building local networks to educate and mobilize citizens. This can involve forming or joining local advocacy groups, holding town hall meetings, and organizing community events.

- **Digital Activism:** Leveraging social media and online platforms to spread awareness, coordinate actions, and apply pressure on policymakers.

- **Coalition Building**: Forming alliances with other groups and organizations to amplify voices and resources. This can include partnerships between civil rights groups, labor unions, environmental organizations, and more.

# Legal and Institutional Resistance

Legal and institutional channels can provide powerful tools for resisting authoritarian measures:

- **Litigation**: Using the courts to challenge unconstitutional or unlawful aspects of Initiative 2025. This involves filing lawsuits, seeking injunctions, and leveraging legal expertise.

- **Policy Advocacy:** Engaging with legislators and policymakers to oppose harmful proposals and promote alternative policies that protect democratic values and social justice.

- **Electoral Participation:** Encouraging voter registration, turnout, and engagement to elect representatives committed to upholding democratic principles and resisting authoritarianism.

# Civic Education and Engagement

Educating and engaging citizens are vital for sustaining a healthy democracy:

- **Civic Education Programs:** Developing and supporting programs that educate citizens about their rights, the importance of democracy, and how they can get involved.

- **Public Awareness Campaigns**: Launching campaigns to raise awareness about the threats posed by Initiative 2025 and the importance of civic participation.

- **Youth Engagement:** Fostering engagement among young people by integrating civic education into school curriculums and providing platforms for youth activism.

# Strategies for Building Resilience

Building resilience within communities and institutions can help withstand authoritarian pressures:

- **Strengthening Local Governance:** Empowering local governments and communities to be more autonomous and resilient against top-down authoritarian measures.

- **Economic Empowerment:** Supporting economic initiatives that promote equity and reduce dependence on centralized power, such as cooperatives and community-based enterprises.

- **Social Cohesion:** Promoting social cohesion through initiatives that bridge divides and foster mutual understanding and cooperation across different communities.

**Expert and Advocate Insights**

I spoke with various stakeholders to gather diverse perspectives on effective resistance strategies:

- **Community Organizers:** Insights from grassroots leaders on the ground about what works and what doesn't in mobilizing local communities.

- **Legal Experts**: Perspectives from constitutional lawyers and civil rights attorneys on the legal avenues available for challenging Initiative 2025.

- **Policy Advocates:** Views from policy experts on how to effectively engage with legislators and influence public policy.

## Mobilizing National and International Support

Building a broad base of support is crucial for effective resistance:

- **National Networks**: Connecting local efforts with national organizations to create a coordinated response, leveraging influence and resources.

- **International Solidarity**: Engaging with global organizations and movements to draw international attention to the threats posed by Initiative 2025, partnering with human rights organizations, and seeking support from foreign governments.

## The Role of Media and Communication

Effective communication strategies are key to spreading the message and mobilizing support:

- **Media Engagement:** Building relationships with journalists and media outlets to ensure coverage of resistance efforts and highlight the dangers of Initiative 2025.

-     **Storytelling:     Crafting** compelling narratives that resonate with the public and humanize the impacts of the proposed changes.

- **Transparency**: Ensuring that resistance efforts are transparent and accountable, building trust and credibility among supporters and the wider public.

## Long-Term Strategies for Sustaining Resistance

Sustaining resistance over the long term requires strategic planning and adaptability:

- **Building Institutional Memory:** Documenting strategies, successes, and challenges to create a knowledge base for future activists.

- **Adaptability**: Being flexible and willing to adjust tactics in response to changing circumstances and new information.

- **Continuous Engagement:** Keeping supporters engaged through regular updates, events, and calls to action to maintain momentum and prevent burnout.

As we face the challenges posed by Initiative 2025, the path ahead will require dedication, resilience, and a deep commitment to democratic principles. The strategies outlined in this chapter provide a roadmap for effective resistance, emphasizing the importance of unity, strategic planning, and sustained engagement.

By learning from past movements, leveraging legal and institutional channels, and mobilizing grassroots and national support, we can build a robust defense against the encroachments of authoritarianism. In doing so, we not only protect our democratic values but also lay the groundwork for a more just and equitable society.

# Conclusion: The Vigilant Path Forward

## Reflecting on the Journey

It is important to reflect on the journey we have taken together. We have delved into the depths of proposed reforms that threaten the democratic fabric of our nation. From the centralization of power and the erosion of civil rights to the dismantling of educational autonomy and the curtailment of free speech, the potential impacts of Initiative 2025 are far-reaching and profound.

## The Stakes for Democracy

Democracy, at its core, is built on the principles of equality, justice, and the rule of law. The threats posed by Initiative 2025 are not just political but moral and ethical. They challenge the very foundation upon which our society is built.

The centralization of power, suppression of dissent, and undermining of civil liberties represent a shift towards authoritarianism that must be resisted.

## The Importance of Vigilance

The price of liberty is eternal vigilance. This age-old adage holds true today more than ever. As citizens, it is our duty to stay informed, engaged, and proactive in defending our democratic values. Vigilance means not only recognizing the threats but also taking action to counter them. It involves being aware of political developments, participating in civic processes, and holding our leaders accountable.

## Strategies for Resistance and Engagement

Throughout this book, we have outlined various strategies for resisting the encroachments of authoritarianism:

- **Grassroots Mobilization:** Building strong, local networks to educate and mobilize citizens.

- **Legal and Institutional Channels**: Using the courts and engaging with policymakers to challenge unconstitutional measures.

- **Civic Education**: Ensuring that citizens understand their rights and the importance of democracy.

- **Media and Communication**: Leveraging the media to inform and mobilize public opinion.

- **Building Resilience:** Strengthening local governance and economic empowerment to withstand authoritarian pressures.

**The Role of Collective Action**

No single individual can protect democracy alone; it requires collective effort. The power of collective action is evident in the historical movements we examined, from the Civil Rights Movement to the anti-apartheid struggle. Unity and solidarity are crucial in facing and overcoming the challenges posed by Initiative 2025.

## A **Call to Action**

In these uncertain times, it is crucial for each of us to remain vigilant and proactive. This book is not just a warning but a call to action—an invitation to stand up for the democratic values that define our nation.

Together, we can ensure that our democracy remains strong and resilient. We must engage with our communities, participate in the political process, and support organizations and movements that advocate for justice and equality.

## **Hope for the Future**

Despite the challenges, there is hope. The resilience and determination of ordinary citizens have historically been the driving force behind significant social and political change. By standing together and refusing to be silenced, we can create a future where democracy thrives, and the rights and freedoms of all individuals are protected.

Let us carry forward the lessons learned and the strategies outlined. Let us remain steadfast in our commitment to democracy and justice. The path ahead may be difficult, but with vigilance, unity, and action, we can protect our democratic values and build a more just and equitable society for future generations.

We can guard the freedom we cherish and ensure a brighter, more democratic future.

www.ingramcontent.com/pod-product-compliance
Lightning Source LLC
Chambersburg PA
CBHW070800250726

48662CB00004B/1905